1001–1580

5 England's Sir Francis Drake sailed for the Pacific in 1577, not for trade but to attack Spain's rich colonies. His *Golden Hind* returned full of treasure in 1580.

6 Portugal's Vasco da Gama made the first voyage to India and back (1497–1499), establishing a rich trading empire.

1001 Leif Eriksson
1492 Columbus
1497 da Gama
1499 Vespucci
1519 Magellan
1577 Drake

the islands of the West Indies, part of a whole "New World"—the American continent. While Spain conquered the West Indies and Central America, Portugal pushed eastward around Africa and by 1515 had seized the valuable spice trade of the East Indies—Europe's first sea-trading empire.

In 1519, Spain sent Ferdinand Magellan to make the first crossing of the Pacific Ocean. He died on the journey, but one of his ships, *Victoria*, completed the first voyage around the world (1519–1522). This exploit was not repeated until Sir Francis Drake's voyage of 1577–1580 in the *Golden Hind*.

ADVENTURES IN THE REAL WORLD

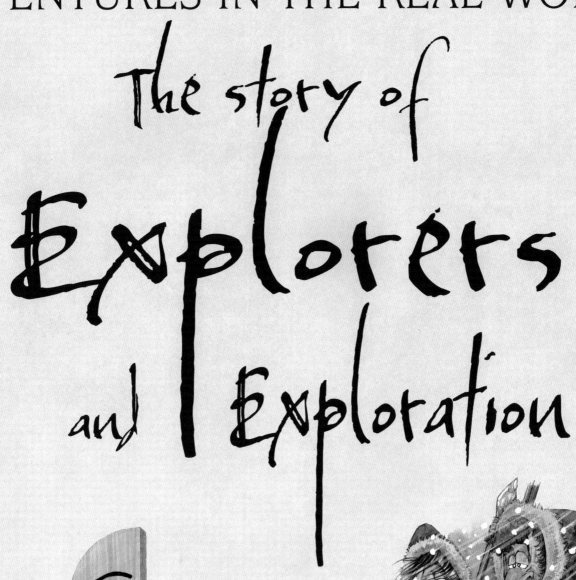

The story of

Explorers

and Exploration

Penny Clarke

Sandy Creek
NEW YORK

Sandy Creek
NEW YORK

An Imprint of Sterling Publishing
387 Park Avenue South
New York, NY 10016

Text © 2013 by The Salariya Book Company Ltd
Illustrations © 2013 by The Salariya Book Company Ltd

This 2013 edition published by Sandy Creek.

Series creator: David Salariya
Author: Penny Clarke
Editor: Stephen Haynes
Illustrations: Dave Antram, Mark Bergin, Mark Peppé, Carolyn Scrace and Gerald Wood
Consultant: Timothy Akers

ISBN 978-1-4351-5031-7 (HB)

Manufactured in Heshan, Guangdong Province, China
Lot #:
2 4 6 8 10 9 7 5 3 1
06/13

Contents

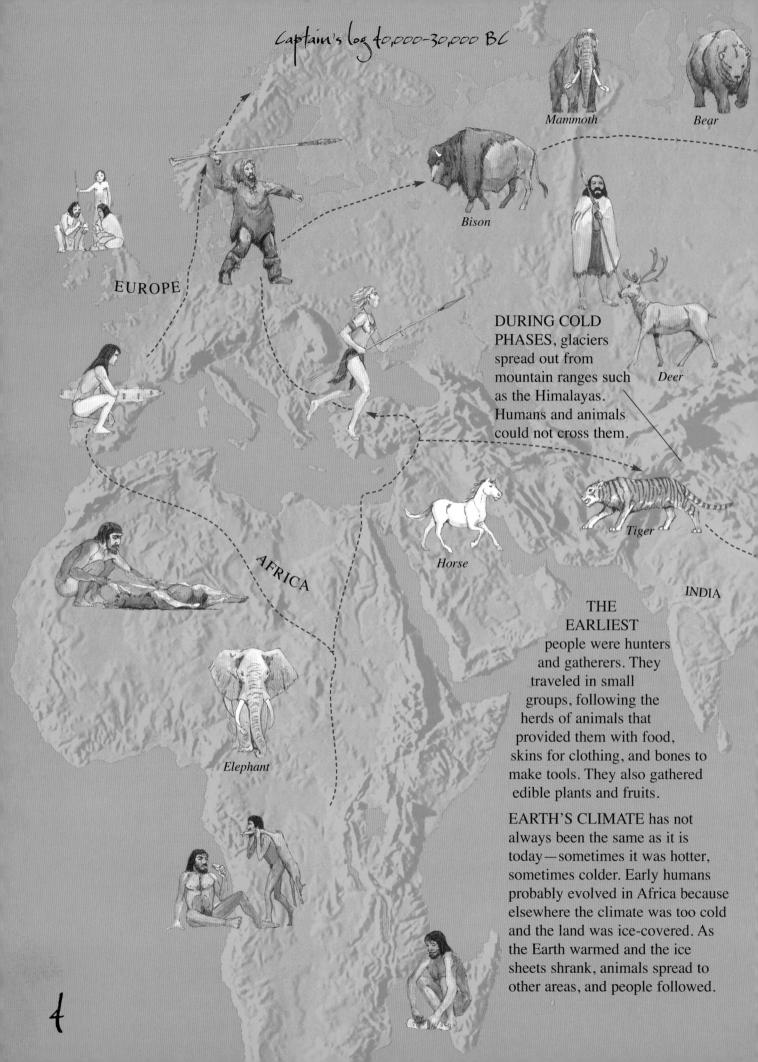

Mammoth

Bear

Bison

EUROPE

Deer

DURING COLD PHASES, glaciers spread out from mountain ranges such as the Himalayas. Humans and animals could not cross them.

Horse

Tiger

AFRICA

INDIA

THE EARLIEST people were hunters and gatherers. They traveled in small groups, following the herds of animals that provided them with food, skins for clothing, and bones to make tools. They also gathered edible plants and fruits.

Elephant

EARTH'S CLIMATE has not always been the same as it is today—sometimes it was hotter, sometimes colder. Early humans probably evolved in Africa because elsewhere the climate was too cold and the land was ice-covered. As the Earth warmed and the ice sheets shrank, animals spread to other areas, and people followed.

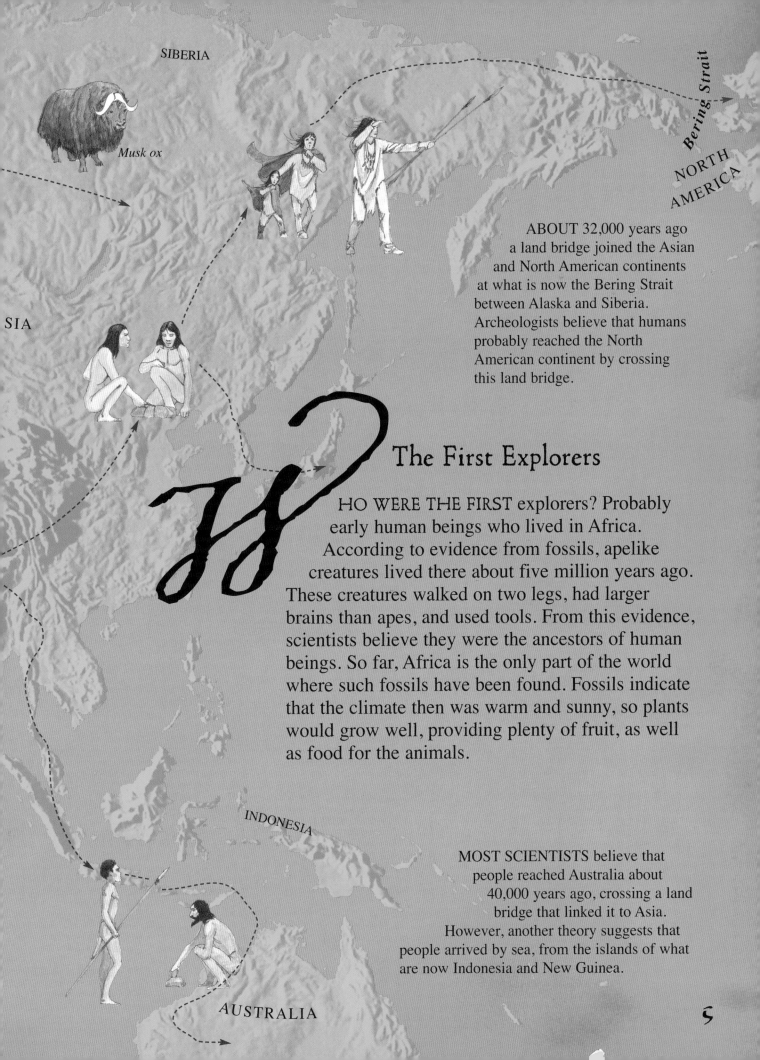

SIBERIA

Musk ox

SIA

NORTH AMERICA

Bering Strait

ABOUT 32,000 years ago a land bridge joined the Asian and North American continents at what is now the Bering Strait between Alaska and Siberia. Archeologists believe that humans probably reached the North American continent by crossing this land bridge.

The First Explorers

WHO WERE THE FIRST explorers? Probably early human beings who lived in Africa. According to evidence from fossils, apelike creatures lived there about five million years ago. These creatures walked on two legs, had larger brains than apes, and used tools. From this evidence, scientists believe they were the ancestors of human beings. So far, Africa is the only part of the world where such fossils have been found. Fossils indicate that the climate then was warm and sunny, so plants would grow well, providing plenty of fruit, as well as food for the animals.

INDONESIA

MOST SCIENTISTS believe that people reached Australia about 40,000 years ago, crossing a land bridge that linked it to Asia. However, another theory suggests that people arrived by sea, from the islands of what are now Indonesia and New Guinea.

AUSTRALIA

THE EGYPTIANS EXPLORE

Akkadian merchants show their king the goods they have brought back.

WITHOUT THE RIVER NILE there would have been no ancient Egyptian civilization. Why? Most of Egypt was dry and arid. But every year, the Nile flooded its banks and left layers of rich silt, which made the land very fertile. Crops grew so well that the ancient Egyptians had plenty to eat, and enough to trade with neighboring people. The Nile was also the best means of transporting goods, as the desert was too hot for people and too rough for most wheeled vehicles. So the river gave the ancient Egyptians produce to sell, and a way to transport it. This allowed Egypt's rulers to build up a powerful state.

Ivory

Baboons

Animal skins

Incense

MADE FROM myrrh and other plant gums, incense was used in religious ceremonies and for embalming dead bodies to make mummies.

Wind and oar power

THIS SEAGOING SHIP was about 80 feet (25 m) long and built of wood. It was powered by a single sail, or by oarsmen.

Manpower

IT TOOK ABOUT 30 men to row this ship. The mast could be lowered when there was no wind.

Myrrh trees

The land of Punt is thought to have been in present-day Somalia.

THE VOYAGE TO PUNT

ARABIA

EGYPT

Red Sea

AFRICA

PUNT?

Hatshepsut

Queen Hatshepsut (1504–1481 BC) is shown here being protected by the god Amun-Re. She sent five ships to Punt in 1493 BC.

The voyage home

THE EGYPTIANS who sailed to Punt found a land where people lived in mud-brick houses set on stilts.

THE EGYPTIANS loaded gold and live baboons onto their ships and set sail for home.

7

THE GREEK EMPIRE

Alexander the Great

TRADE LEADS TO EXPLORATION—or is it the other way around? Certainly the peoples of the eastern Mediterranean were great sailors and traders. To buy tin, the Phoenicians (from present-day Lebanon) probably reached Cornwall, England, around 500 BC. Early Greeks went to the Black Sea to find gold. Later, in the 5th century BC, Hanno the Greek traded along the west coast of Africa. He brought back tales of "hairy women"— probably chimpanzees!

Alexander the Great led his army over huge distances, conquering Persia (present-day Iran) and traveling through Central Asia to India. He died in 323 BC, at age 32, but is still famous for his skill as a military leader.

Phoenicians (700–400 BC)

PHOENICIAN traders sailed all around the Mediterranean, and beyond. Powered by oarsmen and a single sail, their ships could carry a lot of cargo. The Phoenicians were also famous for luxury goods, such as silverware (above).

Alexander the Great

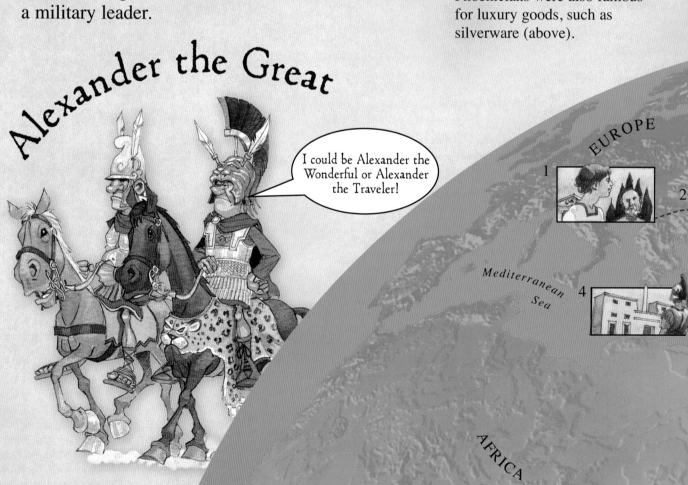

I could be Alexander the Wonderful or Alexander the Traveler!

EUROPE

1

2

Mediterranean Sea

4

AFRICA

We traveled about 15 miles (24 km) each day.

Alexander's travels

1   *334 BC: Alexander sets out from Greece to conquer Asia.*

2   *Defeats strong Persian army at Granicus River.*

3   *332 BC: Marches south; captures rich ports of Tyre and Sidon.*

4   *Goes to Egypt; founds city of Alexandria.*

5   *New war with Persians; goes back to Mesopotamia (present-day Iraq); defeats Persian king Darius at Gaugamela, 331 BC.*

6   *Heads east across wild country chasing Darius.*

7   *330 BC: Darius dies; Alexander marches north; crosses the Khyber Pass, more than 13,000 feet (3,940 m) above sea level.*

8   *328–327 BC: Captures remote kingdom of Bactria; leads army through mountains toward India.*

9   *326 BC: Crosses Indus River. Wants to explore India, but army mutinies.*

10   *Travels west along Indus; proves it is not connected to the Nile.*

11   *Divides his army; some men sail home, others travel by land.*

12   *Marches by night (when cooler) 200 miles (321 km) through hot, barren desert; many men die.*

13   *Fleet short of food and water; mutiny feared. Overland marchers meet fleet at Hormuz; all head inland.*

ASIA

Black Sea

Caspian Sea

5

14

6

7

13

8

9

Persian Gulf

12

ARABIA

10

11

Arabian Sea

Red Sea

INDIA

ROME: THE EMPIRE GROWS

Roman merchant ship

AROUND 900 BC, centuries before Alexander the Great was born, the city of Rome began. It would grow to be the capital of an empire that was larger and longer-lasting than Alexander's. The well-trained Roman army achieved this by conquest, and by good administration of the conquered lands, which allowed trade to flourish. Although the conquered states hated being under Roman control, their merchants welcomed the chance to trade with other parts of the empire. The Roman navy was as powerful as its army, and protected merchant ships from pirates.

Wise men

THE BIBLE tells how "wise men" traveled from the East to Bethlehem to see the newborn Jesus.

Romans abroad!

These barbarians don't seem pleased to see us!

The Roman Empire

The Roman navy

ROMAN galleys were naval ships: they were powered by oarsmen (usually slaves) as well as sails. They were fast and easy to maneuver.

Roman galley

AS THE EMPIRE grew in power and wealth, Roman merchants quickly exploited the ready market for imported goods from China and Central Asia. This network of trade routes reached far beyond the Roman Empire.

Roman roads

paving stones

curbstones

cement

concrete

sand

ditch

groma
(a surveying instrument)

THE ROMANS built good roads throughout their empire so their soldiers could march as quickly as possible. However, merchants soon realized that good roads and direct routes also made transporting goods easier.

Tourism

IN GREECE, Romans visited Athens and, for their health, the temple of Asclepius at Epidaurus.

CROSSING OCEANS

This elegant dish was shipped from China to Iran around AD 800.

CHINESE MERCHANTS BEGAN TRADING with cities along the shores of the Indian Ocean about AD 479. They sold porcelain, silk, and tea, and bought ivory, gold, and spices. In 1403 Emperor Yong Le despatched about 300 ships laden with treasure under Admiral Zheng He. This was a voyage of exploration, and the emperor wished to form alliances with other rulers.

THE VOYAGES OF ZHENG HE

I speak Chinese and Arabic

What languages do you speak, Admiral?

Chinese sailing ships

THIS 15TH-CENTURY Chinese map suggests that Chinese sailing ships had sailed around the southern tip of Africa and reached the Atlantic Ocean.

Cape of Good Hope

Between 1403 and 1424 Zheng He's fleet made seven voyages, visiting many different lands.

CHINA

INDIA

Bay of Bengal

ARABIA

INDIAN OCEAN

China Sea

Chinese sailing vessel

Maori people

AROUND AD 1000, the Maori people reached New Zealand. Centuries earlier their ancestors had left the islands now called Hawaii. Traveling in big oceangoing canoes, they settled the Pacific islands.

BY the 15th century, the biggest Chinese ships were far larger than any European ones. They had crews of 200 men and could carry nearly 1,000 passengers, as well as 1,000 tons of cargo. Columbus crossed the Atlantic with three ships about 65 feet (20 m) long, and he had a total of 120 men.

Pacific islanders

SCATTERED across the Pacific Ocean are thousands of small islands whose inhabitants reached them centuries ago. Between AD 1000 and 1600, the people of Rapa Nui (Easter Island) carved stone figures 40 feet (12 m) high, probably to guard their dead.

VIKINGS: RAIDERS TO TRADERS

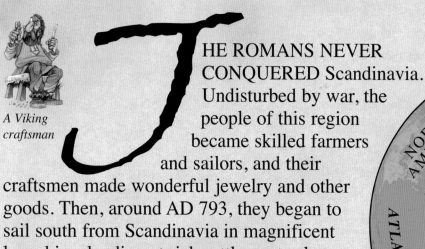

A Viking craftsman

THE ROMANS NEVER CONQUERED Scandinavia. Undisturbed by war, the people of this region became skilled farmers and sailors, and their craftsmen made wonderful jewelry and other goods. Then, around AD 793, they began to sail south from Scandinavia in magnificent longships, landing at rich settlements along the coast. The richest places were generally monasteries, which the Viking raiders looted and burned before returning homeward. Summer became a time of terror for people living near the coasts of England, Ireland, Scotland, and France, as they scanned the horizon for the square-sailed Viking longships.

VIKING SEA ROUTES

NORTH AMERICA

GREENLAND

SCANDINAVIA

ATLANTIC OCEAN

EUROPE

AFRICA

Viking sea routes

- ->

Vikings cross the Atlantic

IN EUROPE Viking raiders met little opposition, but it was different in Vinland (present-day Canada). When Leif Eriksson reached there around AD 1000, all was peaceful. But in AD 1002 Leif's brother Thorwald was killed when he attacked a group of Native Americans.

This turf hut will see us through the winter.

So much for "Vinland" (Wine land) being the land of wine!

Viking merchants

SWEDISH Vikings were traders rather than raiders, selling amber, timber, fish, and furs and buying wine, spices, and silk from the Middle East and southern Europe.

Slaves

Viking ships overland

Vikings traveled east through Russia, sailing mostly on rivers. Between rivers, they dragged their boats overland.

Viking longship

Knorr

Viking ships

VIKING longships were narrow and streamlined, and could be sailed or rowed. All Viking ships had a shallow draft, so could be run ashore easily. Knorrs or merchant ships were shorter and wider, and were used to carry large loads.

Navigation

THE VIKINGS were skillful sailors. They used a device called a navigation table to help them find their way. The needle in the center measured the height of the sun. The navigator could move a bar around the notched edge of the table to plot the ship's course.

VIKING RAIDERS took everything from gold to people. But why return to the cold north when the climate was better farther south? Gradually they began to stay, settle, and marry. So, by around 1100, their descendants had become farmers and craftsmen.

MUSLIM EXPLORERS

Medieval Muslim map of the world, with Mecca at the center

J HE RELIGION OF ISLAM was founded by Muhammad in Arabia around AD 600. Many of his followers traveled widely to spread their faith. Islam encouraged scholarship and learning, and for many centuries Islamic scholars were far more advanced than those in Europe, especially in math, science, and medicine. Many of the ancient Greeks' discoveries survive only because early Islamic scholars recorded them. One scholar, Ibn Fadlan, traveled extensively in northern Russia. His vivid description of a Viking funeral in AD 922 is unique, as the Vikings left few written records. Ibn Battuta (1304–1377) was the greatest Muslim traveler. Born in Tangier, North Africa, he traveled throughout Africa, India, and China.

Route of Ibn Battuta

- - - - - - - - - - - - - - - ->

Ibn Battuta

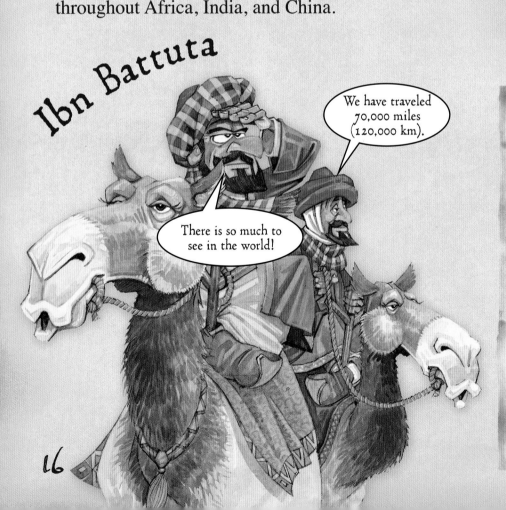

We have traveled 70,000 miles (120,000 km).

There is so much to see in the world!

Al-Idrisi

BORN in North Africa around 1100, al-Idrisi was a great explorer and cartographer. Unfortunately, his greatest achievement, a map of the world engraved on a silver disk, has not survived.

Ibn Fadlan meets the Vikings

Astrolabe c.AD 700

IBN FADLAN tells how a dead Viking chief was put in his longship, together with his weapons, dead horses, and dogs. His favorite slave girl was given a drink which seemed to drug her, and she was taken on board and killed. Finally the ship was set ablaze.

TRAVELING by day in the heat of Arabia is impossible. Instead, explorers traveled by night, navigating by the stars. The astrolabe was invented around AD 700 by Muslim astronomers to help measure the positions of the stars. This made crossing the vast Arabian desert much easier.

Mecca

ALL MUSLIMS should make at least one pilgrimage (hajj) to the city of Mecca. There they visit the Kaaba, Islam's most sacred shrine.

THE OTTOMAN emperors of Turkey employed and encouraged scholars. They studied medicine, astronomy, science, and math, and their magnificent mosques show their technical skills.

Travels by camel

CAMELS provided transportation in the desert lands that most Muslim travelers explored. They can go for a long time without eating or drinking.

MARCO POLO'S TRAVELS

UPON REACHING the Persian Gulf, the Polos continued inland, braving harsh desert winds.

ONE OF THE GREATEST European travelers of the Middle Ages was Marco Polo (1254–1324). He left his home city of Venice in 1271, returning in 1295. In those 24 years he had traveled to China and explored India, Malaysia, and Central Asia. Or had he? Some historians doubt it. He brought back many stories about the exotic places he had seen, and the tales were written down by Rustichello of Pisa, an author of romantic stories. Were these tales exaggerated by either Marco, Rustichello, or both? Some of the things he described seem too fantastic to be true.

Family travels

MARCO'S father and uncle visited China between 1260 and 1269. In 1271 they went again, this time taking Marco too.

Meeting the Pope

AT ACRE (in present-day Israel) the Polos met Pope Gregory. He gave them a letter to give to Kublai Khan, ruler of the Mongols of central Asia.

Hot and cold

TRAVELING conditions were difficult for the Polos. Days were hot, nights cold, and the ground stony and rough. As they went farther east there were also mountain ranges to cross.

Fact or fiction?

Hmmm, I think the khan would like to see you...

20

Kublai Khan

IN 1275 the party reached Kublai Khan's summer palace at Shengdu. The khan questioned the Polos about their travels and he made Marco a roving ambassador—and a spy. Or so Marco later claimed.

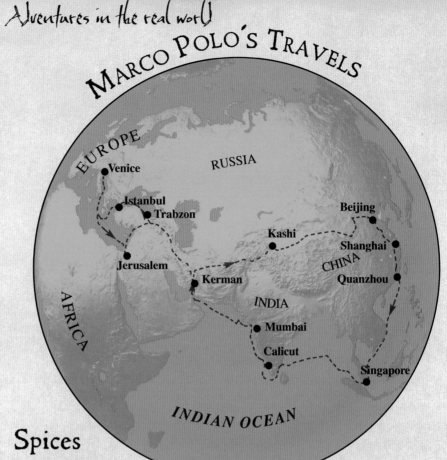

EUROPE

RUSSIA

Venice

Istanbul
Trabzon

Beijing

Kashi

Shanghai

CHINA

Jerusalem

Kerman

Quanzhou

INDIA

Mumbai

Calicut

Singapore

INDIAN OCEAN

Prisoners

KUBLAI KHAN kept the Polos as virtual prisoners for nearly 20 years. He finally agreed they could go—if they escorted Princess Kokachin to her wedding in the Middle East.

Spices

MERCHANTS brought highly valuable spices from the east to Europe.

Cinnamon

Nutmeg

Cloves

Pepper

Reported route of Marco Polo

- - - - - - - - - - - - - - →

CHINESE JUNKS were used to import spices from India and southeast Asia to the Middle East and Europe.

Dog-headed cannibals?

MANY spices came from the Andaman Islands in the Indian Ocean—along with travelers' tales about dog-headed cannibals!

A prisoner again

IN 1298, during a war between Venice and Genoa, Marco Polo was imprisoned by the Genoese. They accused him of lying about his travels.

Home at last

THE POLOS sailed from Trebizond (present-day Trabzon) on the Black Sea to Venice.

1492—AMERICA!

Columbus's coat of arms

IN AUGUST 1492, three ships sailed from Spain commanded by Christopher Columbus. They were heading west, out into the Atlantic Ocean, far beyond the islands of the Azores (discovered in 1418). For centuries, many people had believed the world was flat. (The ancient Greeks knew it wasn't, but that knowledge had been lost.) If the world was flat, going too far from land would mean falling over the edge. But educated people such as King Ferdinand and Queen Isabella of Spain knew better. They funded Columbus's voyage, hoping to find new sources of valuable spices in the East Indies.

Paying for the expedition

If necessary I will sell my jewels to pay for this expedition.

ISABELLA and Ferdinand ruled Spain together. They gave Columbus the money for his voyage.

The "New" World

IN OCTOBER 1492 Columbus landed on the Bahamas. He reached South America on his third voyage and Central America on his fourth.

It's THAT way, I keep telling you!

The world in 1490

THIS MAP, drawn in 1490 by the German scholar Henricus Martellus, shows the countries known to European scholars and sailors. There is, of course, no sign of America.

THE VOYAGES OF CHRISTOPHER COLUMBUS

EUROPE

NORTH AMERICA

Washington, D.C.

SPAIN

Cádiz

ATLANTIC OCEAN

Havana

AFRICA

Santo Domingo

Caracas

SOUTH AMERICA

Lateen to square-rigged

COLUMBUS'S SHIPS were the *Santa Maria*, the *Pinta*, and the *Niña*. He changed their triangular lateen sails, as used in the Mediterranean, to stronger square sails.

Voyage One ----▲----▲---->
Voyage Two ------------->
Voyage Three---•----•---->
Voyage Four --■----■---->

BETWEEN 1492 and 1504 Columbus made four voyages to the so-called "New World." He didn't know he had discovered a continent—he thought he had found a new route to Asia.

The magnetic compass

THE MAGNETIC compass was developed by the Chinese between 55 BC and AD 1064. Arabian scholars had access to it by 1220. The European boxed compass, developed around 1190, made long-distance navigation much easier.

Amerigo Vespucci

ITALIAN NAVIGATOR Amerigo Vespucci moved to Spain when he was 39. He helped to equip the ships for Christopher Columbus's third expedition. He then set sail to South America himself, writing an account of his travels. It was his name that was given to South America, then later to the whole American continent.

I found the way to America? Bah! It was Asia, I tell you!

23

AROUND THE WORLD

Magellan and his crew witnessed the violent storms of the South American coast.

EVEN THOUGH COLUMBUS BELIEVED he had reached Asia, others realized he hadn't. The Portuguese soldier Ferdinand Magellan (1480–1521) was one of them. By 1517 he was sure it was possible to sail around the world by heading west, on a more southerly route than Columbus had taken. In 1519 he set out with a fleet of five ships, paid for by the Spanish king. The voyage was plagued by sabotage, mutinies, and storms. The final disaster was Magellan's death in 1521 on the island of Cebu. Eventually, in September 1522, the *Victoria*, the only remaining ship, returned to Spain. Only about 30 of the original 237 men had survived—the first people to sail around the world and prove Magellan was right.

The Magellan Strait

IT WAS BELIEVED that there was no way to get around the "new" continent lying between Europe and the East Indies. But in October 1520 Magellan discovered a channel linking the Atlantic and Pacific oceans— now called the Magellan Strait.

The Spice Islands

THE RULER of Ternate, one of the Spice Islands, sent his royal barge—a huge outrigger canoe— to look at the *Trinidad* and *Victoria*, the two surviving ships from Magellan's expedition.

The Philippines

THE PHILIPPINES were named in honor of Prince Philip, the king of Spain's son. Without the king's financial help, the voyage would have been impossible.

No plain sailing!

If we go that way, we can be the first around the world.

THE VOYAGES OF MAGELLAN

PACIFIC OCEAN

ASIA

Melanesia

NEW GUINEA

BORNEO

AUSTRALIA

ATLANTIC OCEAN

SPAIN
Seville

AFRICA

SOUTH AMERICA

Rio de Janeiro

Buenos Aires

Puerto San Julian
Magellan Strait

THE EXPLOITS of Magellan and his surviving crew were even greater than those of Columbus. They went farther, even though their ships were of poor quality, and they faced Portuguese attacks in the East Indies and in European waters.

The route taken by Magellan and, after his death, by Juan Sebastián del Cano on their epic voyage.

-------------------------------->

Magellan is killed

THE PEOPLE OF CEBU treated Magellan and his exhausted sailors so well that he agreed to help them in a battle with Mactan islanders. Unfortunately, Magellan was killed in the fighting.

My armor won't save me!

25

CONQUISTADORS ATTACK!

One of de Soto's ships

AFTER COLUMBUS'S 1492 VOYAGE, other Europeans sailed westward. Columbus found little gold, but he returned with stories of people living in golden cities. The Spanish king sent the *conquistador* (Spanish for "conqueror") Hernán Cortés to Mexico to see if these stories were true. The Aztec cities were not golden, but they were full of gold treasures that could be shipped back to Spain. In Peru, the rich Inca civilization was plundered for Spain by Francisco Pizarro. The Spaniards claimed they were bringing Christianity to these people, but this was a flimsy excuse to take their wealth and destroy their civilizations. Within a few years of Cortés landing in Mexico, 90 percent of the Aztecs were killed.

Outgunned

AZTEC WARRIORS believed that Cortés and his followers represented an ancient Aztec priest-king, Quetzalcoatl. When they discovered the truth, it was too late. Their weapons were useless against the firepower of Spanish guns.

Spain takes control

Gulp!

Stop breathing down my neck—aaargh!

Moctezuma

MOCTEZUMA, the ruler of the Aztecs, met with Cortés in 1519.

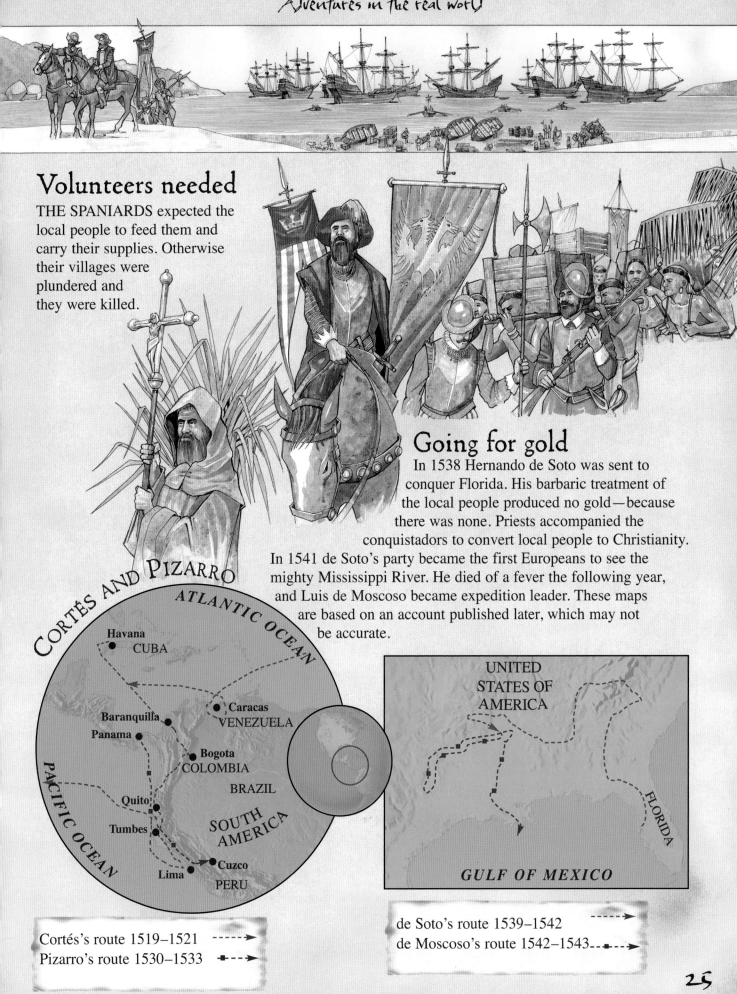

Volunteers needed

THE SPANIARDS expected the local people to feed them and carry their supplies. Otherwise their villages were plundered and they were killed.

Going for gold

In 1538 Hernando de Soto was sent to conquer Florida. His barbaric treatment of the local people produced no gold—because there was none. Priests accompanied the conquistadors to convert local people to Christianity. In 1541 de Soto's party became the first Europeans to see the mighty Mississippi River. He died of a fever the following year, and Luis de Moscoso became expedition leader. These maps are based on an account published later, which may not be accurate.

CORTÉS AND PIZARRO

ATLANTIC OCEAN

Havana
CUBA
Caracas
VENEZUELA
Baranquilla
Panama
Bogota
COLOMBIA
BRAZIL
Quito
Tumbes
SOUTH AMERICA
PACIFIC OCEAN
Lima
Cuzco
PERU

UNITED STATES OF AMERICA
FLORIDA
GULF OF MEXICO

Cortés's route 1519–1521
Pizarro's route 1530–1533
de Soto's route 1539–1542
de Moscoso's route 1542–1543

25

DRAKE AND RALEIGH

Poop

Officers' cabins

Tobacco reached Europe from America in the 16th century.

ENVIOUS OF SPANISH DOMINANCE in the New World, Queen Elizabeth I of England was keen to find a Northwest Passage to the Spice Islands. The country that found this route would become very powerful. Francis Drake—the first Englishman to see the Pacific Ocean—was chosen to command this secret expedition, and on November 15, 1577 he sailed from Plymouth on a journey that would take him around the world. Drake's navigational skills were extraordinary. When he returned, the queen found that her investment of £1,000 in the expedition had brought her £47,000 in return. Drake was allowed to keep £10,000, and was knighted on board his ship, the *Golden Hind*.

Rudder

For Queen and country

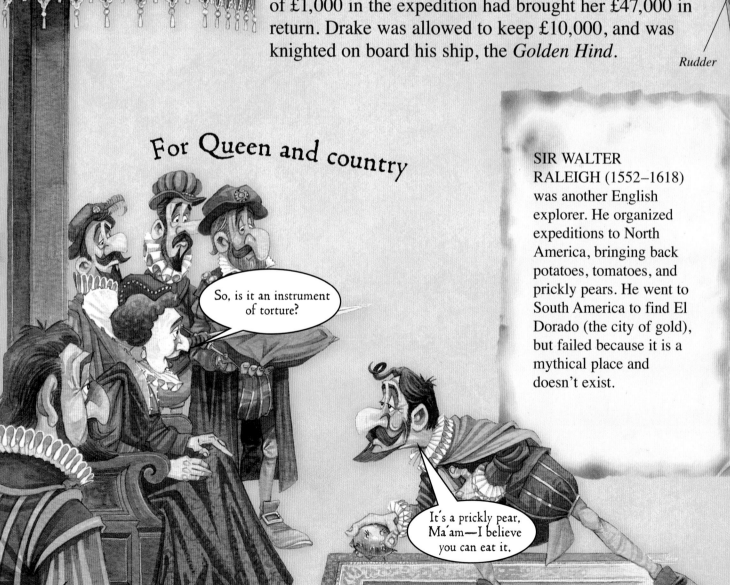

So, is it an instrument of torture?

It's a prickly pear, Ma'am—I believe you can eat it.

SIR WALTER RALEIGH (1552–1618) was another English explorer. He organized expeditions to North America, bringing back potatoes, tomatoes, and prickly pears. He went to South America to find El Dorado (the city of gold), but failed because it is a mythical place and doesn't exist.

Mizzen mast

Rigging

Mainsail

Mainmast

Foresail

Foremast

Boat for going ashore

Bowsprit

Steersman using whipstaff attached to tiller

Stores

Gun deck

Capstan for winding anchor cable

CROSS-SECTION of the Golden Hind, *in which Drake sailed around the world.*

Route taken by Francisco de Orellana

- - - - - - - - - - - - - - - - - - ▶

Exploration of South America

Caracas
VENEZUELA
Georgetown
Bogota
COLOMBIA
Quito
ECUADOR
Manaus
BRAZIL
PERU
Lima
SOUTH AMERICA
BOLIVIA
La Paz

SOUTH AMERICA

South America

SOUTH AMERICA was a magnet for 16th-century explorers seeking gold. In 1542 Francisco de Orellana became the first European to sail up the River Amazon. He returned with tales of warrior women—the fabled Amazons. Walter Raleigh searched for gold farther north, but found neither gold nor Amazons.

GALLEON 1586

Sandglasses were used to tell the time at sea.

JHE GALLEONS OF the late 16th century were steered with a whipstaff—a long lever connected by a hinge (called the gooseneck) to the tiller. The tiller moved the rudder from side to side. The whipstaff was operated by a helmsman, who stood below decks and could not see out.

Sailors

CAPTAINS wanted men with as much sea experience as possible. Sailors were rarely keen to join dangerous voyages, so captains often lied about their destination. By the time the truth was discovered, it would be too late for the sailors to change their minds!

- Shrouds and ratlines
- Forecastle deck
- Swivel guns
- Upper or weather deck
- Weather-deck capstan
- Maindeck
- Mainstay (to mainmast)
- Soldiers at drill
- Beakhead
- Bowsprit step
- Forepeak with stores
- Maindeck capstan
- Foremast step
- Cable tier
- Lower or orlop deck
- Fore cargo stowage
- Provisions in barrels (salt meat and fish, wine, and water)
- Ballast stones in bilge
- Gunner
- Gunner's mate

Area shown in picture above.

Life on board

The smell below decks was terrible—not just from unwashed bodies and clothes, but also from all the ship's waste, which ended up in the bilge with the ballast stones.

Rigging

LONG OCEAN voyages of the 16th century led to changes in ships' rigging.

Fore topgallant sail

Fore topsail

Main topsail

Main topgallant sail

Fore course

Main course

Mizzen and bonaventure sails (triangular or lateen sails)

Bowsprit

Spritsail

Bonnets

Poopdeck

Upper stern gallery

Bonaventure mast

"Great Cabin" for captain or admiral

Helmsman with whipstaff

Mizzen mast

Starboard mizzen shrouds

Starboard main shrouds

Quarterdeck

Maindeck

Upper or weather deck

Stern chaser

Tiller

Gooseneck

Rudder, hung on pintles

Cabin

Area shown in picture above.

Lower or orlop deck

Keel

Sailmaker's store

Hatch to orlop deck

Brick furnace for galley fire, with cauldron for boiling salted meat

Provisions in barrels

Aft capstan

Mizzenmast step

Cook and boy helpers in galley

29

A NEW LIFE

Seal of the first English company to trade in North America, the Virginia Company

AS MORE SHIPS SAILED to and from the New World, navigators and sailors became more experienced—but it was still a dangerous journey. The voyage lasted several months, and waves 40 feet (12 m) high could easily swamp the small wooden ships. But many people were prepared to face such danger— some seeking adventure, some riches, and others prompted by religion. Early in the 16th century King Henry VIII of England broke with the Catholic Church and established the Protestant Church of England. The country changed between Catholic and Protestant under several successive rulers. Persecution was common, and some felt it was safer to risk the dangers of the journey to the New World than to remain in England.

The Algonquians

NATIVE AMERICANS of the Algonquian nation were among the first to have their lands taken from them by European settlers.

Stockades

SSSSSHH! Did you hear that?!

Maybe England would have been safer after all.

THE ALGONQUIANS lived in villages surrounded by stockades, and built homes of saplings, bark, and matting.

SETTLERS BROUGHT European ways with them, including firearms and armor. But armor made it difficult to move through the dense surrounding forests.

The Mayflower

Cargo stored in barrels

Living quarters

Pilgrim Fathers

IN 1620 the *Mayflower* sailed from England with around 100 people on board: the "Pilgrim Fathers." They were going to start a new life free from religious persecution.

IT IS estimated that 35 million Americans—12% of the total population—are direct descendants of those first *Mayflower* Pilgrims.

Attacks

ATTACKS WERE always a danger for villages like Wolstenholme Towne, built upriver from Jamestown, Virginia in 1620. This village prospered, but between 1606 and 1625, more than 6,000 of the 7,000 people who had sailed to a new life in Virginia had died.

Thanksgiving Day

PILGRIM FAMILIES celebrated their first harvest in their new homeland on Thanksgiving Day, 1621. They did not celebrate later harvests—but in 1863 President Abraham Lincoln finally made Thanksgiving Day a permanent holiday in America.

Strong stockade

FRENCH EXPLORERS

Jean Nicolet

JT WAS NOT JUST BRITAIN, Portugal, and Spain who explored and exploited the Americas—French explorers were also there. Etienne Brûlé probably explored the Great Lakes, but left no record of his travels. Others searched for the route to China and the riches that they thought they would find there. In 1634 Jean Nicolet set out to find the "western sea," beyond which he believed he'd find China. No one then had any idea how huge North America is. Nicolet never found his western sea, but he explored the Great Lakes and was the first European to reach the Midwest.

Traders

IN CANADA, Frenchmen called *coureurs de bois* (runners through the wood) traveled great distances to trade with the Native Americans.

THE WINNEBAGO PEOPLE were amazed when they saw Nicolet dressed in a Chinese robe. Like many Europeans, he thought North America was linked to China and it would be tactful to arrive wearing Chinese clothes. But he was actually on Lake Michigan's western shore!

Mistaken identity

I trust I have arrived in China?

No, Lake Michigan!

La Salle names Louisiana and claims it for France.

Louisiana

THE WINNEBAGO had told Nicolet of a great river flowing south: the Mississippi. In 1678 Robert Cavelier de la Salle set out from the Great Lakes to explore the river and reach its mouth. In April 1682 he reached the Gulf of Mexico. He claimed the land he had traveled through for France, and named it Louisiana after King Louis XIV.

SADLY, LOUIS XIV was not impressed. La Salle returned to the Mexican Gulf, where he was murdered in 1684.

THE NIAGARA FALLS, between Lakes Ontario and Erie, blocked la Salle's route. Although the French had heard about the Falls, the sight was still awesome. The expedition carried their boats around the Falls, then continued. In the group was a priest, Louis Hennepin. He spent years exploring in North America, and was captured by Sioux Indians. Later he wrote about his adventures—not always accurately.

COOK IN THE PACIFIC

Maori warriors

I n the 18th century, Europeans knew very little about the South Pacific. The region was thought to contain a giant continent, stretching across the South Pole and reaching as far north as the Tropics. The Solomon Islands, New Zealand, and possibly even Australia were all thought to be part of this huge landmass. Great Britain and France took the lead in exploring the South Pacific. It was the Englishman Captain James Cook, whose three voyages to the South Seas between 1768 and 1779 finally resolved the mystery. His charts of the region, showing the Solomon Islands, New Zealand's North and South Islands, and the east coast of Australia, proved that they were all separate lands.

The Endeavour

Stores

The routes taken by Cook on his three voyages	1768–1771	- - - - -•- - - -•- - - ▸
	1772–1775	- - - - -■- - - -■- - - ▸
	1776–1779	- - - - - - - - - - - - ▸

Wardroom

Barrels of fresh water

Living quarters

THE *ENDEAVOUR*, Cook's ship, had originally carried coal. It was strongly built and could carry 660 tons of cargo and crew—essential for the sort of expedition Cook was planning. He also needed space for the specimens he hoped to collect.

A globe that opens to show the positions of the stars and constellations.

A portable observatory

COOK took a portable observatory so he could study the stars, and in 1769 he observed a rare phenomenon: the transit of Venus across the Sun.

EUROPEANS EXPLORE AFRICA

Many slaves were taken from Africa at this time

EUROPEANS HAVE BEEN TRADING with Africa for centuries, but until the 19th century, trade was only with coastal areas and lands north of the Sahara. The climate and geography made further exploration extremely difficult. In areas with high rainfall there was dense jungle, and in drier regions there was scrub. There were high mountains, deep valleys, and dangers ranging from big cats to tiny, disease-carrying insects. Waterfalls and rapids often made large rivers impassable, and many of the local people were understandably hostile to outsiders. But, as more of the Earth was explored, Africa and its unknown interior began to arouse interest.

A 16th-century map of Africa drawn by Descalier, a French geographer. Based on sailors' reports, it is very accurate.

The River Niger

MUNGO PARK (1771–1806), a Scottish doctor, made the first scientific exploration of the River Niger in West Africa. He was drowned during an ambush.

Into Africa

Timbuktu

TALES OF TIMBUKTU tantalized European explorers. In 1826, Scotsman Alexander Laing (left) was first to reach the city. He was murdered soon afterward. The Frenchman René-Auguste Caillié (right) was luckier—he got there in 1827 and survived.

CAMEL TRAINS transported goods such as salt, gold, cloth, and slaves across the Sahara. They were also the only way for Europeans to cross the Sahara—but not without danger.

Routes taken by some European explorers of Africa in the 19th century

Park	- - - - - - - - - - →
Caillié	- • - • - • - • - →
Laing	- ■ - ■ - ■ - →
Burton and Speke	- - - ‹ - ‹ - →
Speke and Grant	············→
The Bakers	‹ - ‹ - ‹ - →

The source of the River Nile

SEVERAL EXPEDITIONS had tried, but failed, to find the Nile's source. In 1859 Englishman John Speke (left) thought he had found it, but fellow explorer Richard Burton (right) disagreed. Speke tried again, this time with James Grant. In July 1862 Speke was indeed proved correct.

AS THEY returned, Speke and Grant found the explorers Samuel and Barbara Baker waiting for them. The Bakers would become the first Europeans to see the Kabarega Falls in present-day Uganda.

The Bakers at the Kabarega Falls

DOCTOR LIVINGSTONE?

Dr. David Livingstone

JWO OF THE BEST-KNOWN 19th-century explorers of Africa are David Livingstone (1813–1873), a Scottish doctor, and Henry Stanley (1841–1904), a Welsh journalist. In 1841 Livingstone went to southern Africa as a missionary. In 1848 he decided to explore the central part of Africa, and was the first European to see many of its magnificent sights, including the great waterfalls on the Zambezi River, which he named the Victoria Falls, after the British queen. By 1871 no one had heard from him for three years. Sensing a good story, the editor of the *New York Herald* sent Henry Stanley, the paper's European correspondent, to find Dr. Livingstone.

Mary Livingstone

MARY MOFFAT (1820–1862) married David Livingstone in 1845. The following years were difficult for her, with frequent moves and illnesses. She had six children, and sometimes suffered from partial paralysis. She and the children returned to England for four years in order for her to recover. After her death in 1862, Livingstone continued his missionary work for 11 more years.

The Zambezi River

You're not looking at lunch!

SUSA AND CHUMAH were Livingstone's servants but soon became his friends. They traveled with him on many of his expeditions.

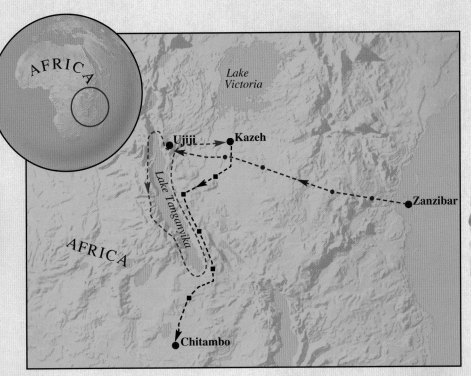

THE JOURNEYS made by Livingstone and Stanley, separately and together, between 1871 and 1873. Stanley's group took several months to travel the 2,100 miles (3,500 km) from Zanzibar to Ujiji.

Stanley	----•----•----•----→
Livingstone	----■----■----■----→
Stanley and Livingstone	----------→

"Dr. Livingstone, I presume"

STANLEY FOUND Livingstone on November 10, 1871 in the trading town of Ujiji by Lake Tanganyika, and it made him famous. Livingstone's many years of exploring had damaged his health, and he was often too weak to walk. But he refused to return to England with Stanley, preferring to remain in Africa. Livingstone treated his African helpers well, and many were devoted to him. When he was found dead in May 1873, his servants buried his heart in Africa, then carried his body hundreds of miles to the coast in a journey that took nine months. Livingstone was given a state funeral in Westminster Abbey, London, on April 18, 1874.

Medical supplies

ILLNESS WAS one of the greatest threats facing Europeans in Africa. Every expedition had to take its own medical supplies. This is Stanley's medical chest.

Henry Morton Stanley

Dr. David Livingstone

39

WOMEN EXPLORERS

Mary Kingsley

ON 19TH-CENTURY EUROPE women's lives were usually restricted to marrying and having children. They were not expected to be explorers. But some women did indeed explore Africa: Dutch Alexine Tinne explored the Nile south of Khartoum, American-born May French-Sheldon led an expedition to Mount Kilimanjaro, and Englishwoman Mary Kingsley explored west and equatorial Africa. Born in 1862, Kingsley lived quietly with her parents for 30 years, but when they died, she went to Africa. She made two expeditions, from June to December 1893 and again from December 1894 to November 1895. She made so many discoveries and won so much respect that she was appointed an adviser to the British government. She died, only 38 years old, working as a nurse in South Africa during the Boer War.

The Fang people

KINGSLEY LIVED with the Fang people, who built their villages near the Ogooué River, in present-day Gabon. She studied their culture and thought it should be protected from European ways. She gave this carving of a Fang girl (below) to the British Museum in London.

Kingsley's visiting card

I wonder who will find it . . .

MARY KINGSLEY collected many specimens for the British Museum: 65 different species of fish, and 18 different species of reptile. Most were preserved in alcohol.

Snoutfish (in alcohol)

AFRICA

Lake Chad

Lake Volta

Elmina   Calabar   ▲ Mount Cameroon

ATLANTIC OCEAN

Matatdi

Boma

Luanda

AFRICA

KINGSLEY WROTE a book and gave talks in Britain about her experiences. Once, atop Mount Cameroon, an active volcano 13,432 feet (4,095 m) high, she left her visiting card under a stone (opposite page).

Journeys of Mary Kingsley
1893 ------•------•------•----➤
1894 ----------------------➤

IN HER BOOK *Travels in West Africa* Kingsley describes an encounter with a crocodile. She scared it away from her canoe with "a clip on the snout with the paddle," then paddled away as fast as she could.

43

FROM COAST TO COAST

Indian basket and rattle

IN 1763, after a successful military expedition, Britain took over France's lands in Canada. Slowly the British explored farther west. News came that Captain Cook had been to Canada's west coast and found there was a market in China for Canadian furs. East-coast companies wanted a share of the trade, but needed an overland route. In 1789 Alexander Mackenzie was sent to find one, but the river he found (now named the Mackenzie) flowed into the Arctic Ocean. In 1792, after another very difficult journey, he finally succeeded. It took five weeks to reach the source of the Peace River in the Rockies. One river (now the Fraser) was too dangerous for canoes, so Mackenzie and his party went on foot—through snow, forests, and over mountains—before finding a river that flowed to the Pacific.

IN 1808 Simon Fraser explored the river that Mackenzie had found too dangerous for canoes. The only way to get around some steep cliffs was on Native American ladders made of roots and bark, which swayed alarmingly in the wind.

The Pacific

I've done it—I've reached the Pacific!

ARCTIC OCEAN

USA

Inuvik

Great Slave Lake

Hudson Bay

Rocky Mountains

PACIFIC OCEAN

CANADA

UNITED STATES OF AMERICA

Carved in stone

"ALEX MACKENZIE from Canada by land 22nd July 1793." Mackenzie carved this inscription on a rock near the Pacific Ocean to mark his achievement. It is still there, now preserved in red concrete.

MACKENZIE'S PARTY lost most of their supplies when their canoes capsized.

THE ROCKY MOUNTAINS had always stopped French and British fur traders from crossing Canada. When Mackenzie reached the Pacific in July 1793, he became the first European to cross North America from coast to coast.

Journeys of Mackenzie
1789 -------•-------•-------•-------→
1793 -----------------------------→

EUROPEAN EXPLORERS of North America relied heavily on Native Americans for local knowledge and to act as guides. Native Americans adapted their lives to their surroundings: those who lived in the dense forests were mostly hunters and trappers, while those on the plains were expert horsemen.

LEWIS AND CLARK

Fur traders

SINCE LA SALLE'S TIME (see page 33), Lousiana had remained largely unexplored. In 1803 the French emperor Napoleon sold the territory to America—the "Louisiana Purchase." President Thomas Jefferson wanted an easy trade route to the Pacific coast. He chose two army officers, Meriwether Lewis and William Clark, to lead an expedition. They set off up the Missouri River in 1804, spending a bitter winter near a Mandan village in North Dakota. After many months of dangerous travel (horses fell over precipices and food was running out), the expedition reached the Pacific on October 16, 1805.

Trappers

THE FIRST European explorers of North America were fur trappers. Associations of merchants, such as the Hudson's Bay Company of Canada, built well-defended trading posts such as Fort Garry. Many of these later grew into towns.

The call of the wild

On June 13, 1805 Lewis escaped from a grizzly bear by swimming a river.

You don't seem pleased to see me!

Lewis and Clark

Lewis (left) (1774–1809) and Clark (right) (1770–1838) made a good team. Lewis was a scholar, interested in scientific observation. Although a brilliant organizer, he was a quiet and rather distant man. Clark, however, was much more outgoing and an excellent second-in-command. Lewis later became Governor of Louisana.

CANADA

Rocky Mountains

Louisiana Territory

Journey of Lewis and Clark across the Rocky Mountains

-------------------------→

WHEN LEWIS AND CLARK left North Dakota they employed a Canadian *coureur de bois* (see page 32) who brought his Shoshone wife, Sacajawea.

Crossing the Rocky Mountains, they entered Shoshone lands. The chief was Sacajawea's brother. The Shoshone's help and advice allowed the expedition to

avoid some extremely dangerous rivers and reach the Pacific coast in safety.

A SPIRIT DANCE by Native Americans of the northwest coast. In their journals Lewis and Clark made valuable notes and observations on Native American life.

A CHINOOK CHIEF met the party by the mouth of the Columbia River, down which they traveled to the Pacific. Sacajawea did not speak his language, and so interpreted with signs.

45

THE WAY TO THE WEST

Settlers and gold prospectors followed dangerous cross-country trails.

THE ROUTE FOUND by Lewis and Clark was far too difficult for regular travel. In February 1824 a party of trappers led by Jedediah Smith was traveling west when snow blocked their way. A Crow Indian told them of a more southerly route through the mountains. Smith and his party realized this was the ideal route to the west—they called it the South Pass.

CANADA

▲ Frémont Peak
○ South Pass

UNITED STATES
OF AMERICA

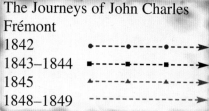

The Journeys of John Charles Frémont

Year	
1842	●---●---●---→
1843–1844	■---■---■---→
1845	▲---▲---▲---→
1848–1849	---------→

TALES OF fortunes to be made in the west soon spread, and many people set out on the dangerous journey. But as yet there were no maps or marked routes. In 1842 the US government appointed army surveyor John Charles Frémont to map out the best routes.

If you want to travel far and fast, travel light!

48

Wrong mountain!

FRÉMONT'S nickname was "the Great Pathfinder." His books about his expeditions sold in huge numbers. He climbed the "highest" peak in the Rockies, planting the American flag on the summit. It was a popular gesture, but he had chosen the wrong peak —there are higher ones!

California

IN 1845 Frémont's mapping work was interrupted by war between the United States and Mexico. The unequal conflict didn't last long. Mexico lost California, which became the 31st state of America, and Frémont was appointed military governor. He became a millionaire after the gold rush of 1848, and was even nominated for the presidency in 1856.

Pyramid Lake

ALTHOUGH MUCH of Frémont's work was mapping sites that had already been discovered, he did make some new discoveries, including Pyramid Lake in Nevada.

ACROSS AUSTRALIA

Australia and Tasmania

CAPTAIN COOK HAD REPORTED good farming land in the area around Sydney. Unfortunately for the first settlers, he was wrong. Not until 1813 did British explorers find a way through the Great Dividing Range to the really fertile land beyond. Slowly, settlements grew up along the coast, but the searing heat of Australia's desert interior made it difficult to cross. Many explorers died in the attempt, including Robert Burke and William Wills. Camels were imported from Asia to carry explorers' equipment across the interior, as they are well adapted to high temperatures, little water, and sandy terrain. They thrived, and there are still wild camels in Australia today.

Burke and Wills

ROBERT O'HARA Burke (left) (1820–1861) led the first known expedition to cross Australia from south to north. His party left in August 1860, but by February 1861 they could go no farther and turned back. Burke, William Wills (right) (1834–1861), and John King returned to a deserted camp at Cooper's Creek. Exhausted and starving, Burke and Wills died in June 1861, but King survived and was rescued.

Surviving the desert

I need to change you for a camel!

48

EUROPEAN explorers had problems with the climate, but Australia's native Aboriginal people had no such difficulties. Skilled trackers, they knew how and where to find food and water in the continent's dry wastes. Many expeditions employed them as guides.

Route of Burke and Wills's journey across Australia

- - - - - - - - - - - - - - - - - - ➤

AUSTRALIA'S CLIMATE is harsh, so the Aboriginal people moved around to find food and water. But European settlers did not understand this, and drove them off the land the settlers were trying to farm, which caused conflict.

Adelaide

NAMED AFTER Queen Adelaide, consort of the British king William IV, the city was founded in 1836 as the capital of the province of South Australia. It was the starting point for many early expeditions into the Australian desert.

THE ABORIGINAL people have many sacred places in Australia's interior, where they hold special ceremonies.

TO THE NORTH POLE

Captain's log AD 1500–1930

Husky team

COLUMBUS'S DISCOVERY OF AMERICA was exciting, but traders really wanted a westward route to Asia. So the search was on for a way around the "new" continent. Magellan's southern route (see pages 22–23) was a long and difficult voyage. There was a northern route, but this was very dangerous, and was frozen for much of the year. Explorers also realized that there was an area around the North Pole that never thawed. So, in the 19th century, various governments started funding scientific expeditions to reach the North Pole.

Destination Asia?

IN 1576 Martin Frobisher, an English explorer searching for the Northwest Passage, reached Baffin Island. The facial features of the Inuit people there made him think he had reached Asia.

Baffin Island
Hudson Bay
CANADA
Hudson Estuary

Cartier 1534
Cartier 1535–1536
Frobisher 1576
Hudson 1609
Hudson 1610–1611

Journeys by early explorers searching for a northerly route around North America.

Spears and bows are no match for our muskets.

FROBISHER and his men had a few skirmishes with the people of Baffin Island.

Trapped in the Arctic

Lookout and chimney

Cabin built of ship's timber

Furniture from the trapped ship

Barents's journey 1596

Amundsen's route 1903–1906

Peary's expedition 1909

TRADE HAD LED TO the search for the Northwest Passage in the 16th century, but national pride was behind the race to the North Pole.

Willem Barents (died 1597)

IN 1596 DUTCHMAN Willem Barents's ship was trapped by the Arctic ice. His party built a cabin and survived the winter, but he died on the voyage home.

ROBERT PEARY (1856–1920), an American naval officer, was the first to reach the North Pole in 1909—it was his eighth attempt.

CHARLES HILL (1821–1871), another American, made three unsuccessful attempts to reach the North Pole. He died on the third.

NORWEGIAN EXPLORER Roald Amundsen took an easier way to the North Pole in 1928—by airship!

Captain's log AD 1910-1914

RACING SOUTHWARD

O NCE THE NORTH POLE had been reached, the new challenge was the South Pole. Captain Robert Falcon Scott (1869–1912) had led the first British investigations of Antarctica in 1901–1914. On his second expedition, between 1910 and 1912, he intended to go to the South Pole. However, the Norwegian explorer Roald Amundsen, using Inuit methods learned in the Arctic, got there first. Amundsen's team chose a route along the narrow Axel Heiberg Glacier and headed for the Pole with plenty of supplies. Scott's journey was plagued by bad weather and his men died of cold and exhaustion on their way back to base camp.

Shackleton's ship, the Endurance

Endurance

CRASSH!

Abandon ship!

Captain Robert Falcon Scott

SCOTT STARTED his ascent of Antarctica's Beardmore Glacier on December 10, 1911. His team arrived at the South Pole on January 18, 1912, only to find that Amundsen had beaten them. The weather on the return journey was savage, and blizzards made travel impossible. Scott was the last of the party to die, only 11 miles (17 km) from his destination, on March 29, 1912.

Endurance against all the odds!

IN 1914 British explorer Ernest Shackleton (1874–1922) tried to cross Antarctica via the South Pole. After his ship, *Endurance*, was crushed in the ice, the crew had to take to the lifeboats. They traveled more than 900 miles (nearly 1,500 km) through icy storms to reach land. Shackleton and two crewmen traveled the last 140 miles (240 km) alone to raise a rescue party for their stranded shipmates. The whole crew survived.

Expedition of Amundsen ●------►
Expedition of Scott ------►
(Both 1911–1912)

AMUNDSEN had learned a lot from the Inuit. He used huskies to haul his team's sleds, while Scott used ponies. Like the Inuit, Amundsen's men wore clothes made from reindeer and seal skins, which were light and warm. Scott's party wore heavier clothing, which kept them neither warm nor dry.

EVEN THOUGH Scott's ponies came from the cold region of Manchuria in China, some died in the intense Antarctic cold; the rest had to be shot.

Scott's pony team

WITHOUT PONIES, Scott's team had to pull the sleds themselves. Exhaustion probably contributed to their deaths.

The huskies Amundsen had brought from Greenland to pull his sleds thrived in the cold of the Antarctic.

First to the South Pole

ROALD AMUNDSEN (1872–1928) dreamed of reaching the North Pole first. He was just setting out when he heard that Robert Peary was already there. So he headed for the South Pole instead, reaching his goal on December 14, 1911. He rested for three days before starting the journey back.

Map labels: SOUTH ATLANTIC OCEAN, Weddell Sea, Queen Maud Land, Bellingshausen Sea, ANTARCTICA, SOUTHERN OCEAN, South Pole, Marie Byrd Land, SOUTH PACIFIC OCEAN, Amundsen Sea, Ross Sea, George V Land, Wilkes Land

BELOW THE WAVES

Early diving suit invented by August Siebe, 1819

AS MORE AND MORE of the Earth was explored, there remained one huge and almost unknown region. What lay below the world's oceans? The many myths about sea monsters showed people's fascination for the undersea world—but they didn't have the technology to go there. The deepest oceans are difficult to explore: light cannot penetrate that far down, making it dark and cold. The water pressure is so great that without strong, reinforced hulls, deep-sea craft would be crushed.

Diving bell

Lead sheets

Barrels to replenish the air

Ballast weights

SIR EDMUND HALLEY'S diving bell of 1690. Air trapped inside enabled men to work on the seabed.

Alvin
A submersible for deep-sea research

Oarfish

In deep water strong lights are essential.

Rattail fish

Asia
North America
Europe
Asia
Pacific Ocean
Atlantic Ocean
Africa
South America
Indian Ocean
Australasia
Antarctic Ocean

THE VOYAGES of *Challenger*, the first deep-sea exploration ship (1872–1876).

Camera extends up to 200 ft (60 m) from craft.

Viperfish

Hatchetfish

JACQUES COUSTEAU invented the aqualung in 1943. Cylinders of compressed air are strapped onto a diver's back. The air is breathed through a special valve. Another name for the device is "scuba," which stands for **S**elf-**C**ontained **U**nderwater **B**reathing **A**pparatus.

Aqua-Lung™

The bathyscaphe

THE BATHYSCAPHE was invented by Belgian explorer Auguste Picard.

Bathyscaphe

PICARD'S *TRIESTE*, with its crew of two, took eight hours to reach the bottom of the Mariana Trench—the deepest spot on Earth at 36,000 feet (11,000 m)—in 1960. The craft was subjected to immense pressure.

Spherical crew compartment

Extra-thick steel walls

Textile II, oil exploration vehicle

IN TODAY'S DIVING SUITS of strengthened metal, a diver can work about 650 feet (200 m) below the sea's surface. Inside the suit the air pressure is normal. For deep diving, suits have been developed which allow for depths of up to 2,300 feet (700 m).

Mariana Trench

EXPLORING SPACE

Apollo 13

SPACE EXPLORATION is difficult because of the huge distances involved. Some planets are so far away that the light waves from them were first transmitted when dinosaurs still roamed the Earth! By the mid-20th century, new technology finally made space exploration possible. Scientists in America and the USSR had developed rocket technology—first used by Germany in World War II—to blast spacecraft beyond the pull of the Earth's gravity.

Moon landing 1969

I'd better collect plenty of moon rock—who knows if we'll be back?

First man in Space

YURI GAGARIN (1934–1968), a Soviet cosmonaut, became the first man in space, orbiting the Earth one and a half times in 1961.

Orbit

Craft lands

Reentry

EARTH

Launch

Gagarin lands

Orbit

Spacecraft

Rocket

The Vostok *rocket that blasted Gagarin into space was more than 100 ft (30 m) high.*

"One giant leap for mankind"

IN 1961 American President John F. Kennedy declared his commitment to land a man on the Moon within the next decade. In 1969 this became reality, and television viewers around the world watched Neil Armstrong and Buzz Aldrin walk on the Moon's surface.

THE FIRST lunar missions were called *Apollo* after the Greek god who was the guardian of travelers.

Command module

Service module

Lunar module

Third stage

Second stage

First stage

The Saturn rocket that took the Apollo Moon expedition into space in 1969.

THE ASTRONAUTS landed on the Moon in the lunar excursion module. Then they used the battery-powered lunar roving vehicle for exploring. Men and machines had to work in extreme temperatures and very low gravity.

Shuttles

SPACE EXPLORATION is enormously expensive. To reduce the costs, the Space Shuttle, a reusable spacecraft, was designed. It was taken into space by a pair of booster rockets. In space it used small rocket motors to maneuver. Back in Earth's gravity, it flew like a glider.

External fuel tank

Booster rockets

Space Shuttle

ROBOTS TO MARS!

Mars Pathfinder

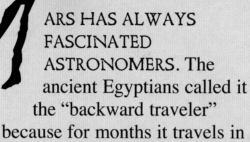

MARS HAS ALWAYS FASCINATED ASTRONOMERS. The ancient Egyptians called it the "backward traveler" because for months it travels in one direction and then suddenly appears to travel backward. The Romans called it Mars after their god of war.

Early telescopes were not very powerful, which led to many incorrect ideas about the planet's surface, including the belief that it was crisscrossed by irrigation canals. *Mars Global Surveyor* was launched in 1996 to carry out a long-term study from an orbit around the planet. In its first three years, *MGS* returned more data that all previous Mars missions combined, including high-resolution images of the so-called "face on Mars."

Viking probes 1975

ONLY ROBOTS can explore Mars—no human could survive there without specially developed suits. In 1975 two *Viking* probes (right) landed on the planet. They collected rocks and sent back color pictures, but found no signs of life.

MARINER 9 orbited Mars every 12 hours for nearly a year in 1971. It sent back pictures showing a dust storm covering the entire planet. When the storm ended the craters of four huge volcanoes were visible.

IN 1971 the USSR's *Mars 3* captured the first panorama of the planet's surface. But it was photographs taken by the American *Mariner 9* during 1971 and 1972 that gave the first really clear information about the planet's surface.

MORE RECENT investigations have suggested that there may have been water on Mars in the distant past. The Mars rover *Curiosity* landed in 2012 to carry out further studies of the Martian climate.

Pathfinder's target landing area

Ares Vallis

Landing site

Cruise-stage separation

Parachute deployed at 760 mph (1,226 km/h)

Heat-shield separation

The sequence of events as Pathfinder touched down on Mars on July 4, 1997, landing in a valley called Ares Vallis.

Airbags start to inflate at 150 mph (241 km/h)

Retro-rocket ignition and release

Pathfinder bounces and rolls to a halt. Air bags deflate and solar panel petals open

THE *MARS PATHFINDER* landed on Mars in 1997 after a journey of seven months covering 308 million miles (496 million km). It landed without orbiting Mars first to slow down. Its descent began 80 miles (128 km) above the planet's surface, traveling at 16,740 mph (27,000 km/h). Touching down, it bounced along on huge airbags before stopping. When the bags deflated, solar panels opened out.

WHEN *PATHFINDER*'S SOLAR PANELS OPENED, *Sojourner*, a rover vehicle 11 inches (28 cm) high, was released. It was powered by solar panels and had instruments for studying the Martian surface.

Imager for Mars Pathfinder (IMP)—a stereoscopic camera

PATHFINDER

UHF antenna

Solar panels

Instruments to analyze soil and rock

SOJOURNER

Rover ramp

59

A FUTURE IN SPACE?

Artist's impression of a spacecraft landing on Mars

SURPRISINGLY, THE REAL PROBLEM with space exploration lies not with technology, but cost. Exploring with probes and other robots is useful, but limited. Humans make the best explorers, but at present they cannot survive conditions on Mars, the planet likely to be explored first. However, travel to the Moon once seemed beyond the realms of possibility too, so perhaps humans will be able to explore further in the future.

TRAVELING TO Mars would take at least six months— manned spacecraft are heavier than robot probes.

Astronauts will explore in a rover vehicle like this

The huge distance to travel here means that we will be away from Earth for at least three years.

SCOTT

THE INTERNATIONAL SPACE STATION (ISS) was designed as a cooperative effort among 16 countries including Russia, Japan, the USA, and the members of the European Space Agency. Launched on November 20, 1998, and orbiting 209 miles (354 km) above Earth, it carries a crew of six and weighs around 450 tons. The ISS is expected to remain in use until at least 2020.

Space colonies

IN THE 1970s American scientists began to design a space colony that could replicate conditions on Earth. It would have gravity, seasons, plants, and water, and could be used if Earth became uninhabitable.

Living in space

THE BIGGEST challenge for astronauts is staying alive. Once on Mars, they would need to stay there until its orbit aligned with Earth's again—which happens every 18 to 24 months. Research on living in space is already underway at the Johnson Space Center, Texas. A Mars Habitat Testbed Module is part of the International Space Station, and will provide a better understanding of long-term space travel.

GLOSSARY

Akkadians people from Akkad, a kingdom which flourished around 3500 BC in what is now Iraq.

align to be in line; used to refer to the position of planets.

archeologist a person who studies human history by looking at the physical remains of the past.

arid very dry and unsuitable for growing plants.

Assyria the state which dominated much of what is now Iraq from about 1500 to 650 BC.

astronomer a scientist who studies space and the objects in it, such as planets.

barbarian an uncultured, uncivilized person.

bilge the lowest part of a ship's hull.

cartographer a person who draws maps.

conquistadors military commanders sent by the rulers of Spain to conquer America (the "New World").

embalming a way of preserving dead bodies.

evolve to change over a long period of time and become better suited to your surroundings.

fossils preserved remains of ancient living things.

incense perfume burned during religious ceremonies.

irrigation an artificial method of taking water to fields and crops.

isthmus a narrow strip of land joining two larger areas.

khan ruler of the Mongols.

longships the Vikings' long, narrow warships, powered by oarsmen and sails.

Low Countries the region of northwest Europe covering modern Belgium, the Netherlands, and Luxembourg.

Middle Ages a period of European history, roughly from AD 1000 to 1453.

Mongols a nomadic people who lived in Central Asia.

myrrh a strong-smelling resin obtained from trees, used to make perfumes.

mythical not really existing, except in myths and legends.

orbit the regular path taken by one object around another. For example, the Earth orbits the Sun.

Ottomans the powerful rulers of the Turkish empire between the 15th and 19th centuries.

pack animal an animal that carries goods on its back.

prow the front of a boat.

silt very fine earth carried by a river. When the river slows, or floods, the silt is deposited on the ground or the riverbed.

source the place where a river begins.

Soviet coming from the USSR.

Spanish Main the area of land and sea in and around the Caribbean that was controlled by Spain in the 16th century.

stockade a strong defensive fence, usually wooden, around a homestead or fort.

strait a narrow stretch of sea linking two larger seas.

USSR (Union of Soviet Socialist Republics) a group of countries once ruled as a single state by the Russian government in Moscow. Most of these countries are now part of the Commonwealth of Independent States.

visiting card a small card printed with a person's name and address. In Victorian and Edwardian times middle- and upper-class people left a card if they visited someone but found they were not at home.

INDEX

THE NAVIGATOR

The three Ls

Landmarks

Log line

Lead line

ON LONG OCEAN VOYAGES the skills of the navigator were vital. If he got his sums wrong and plotted a faulty position or course, the whole crew could die of thirst and hunger far out at sea.

In familiar waters, close to land, the navigator used the "three Ls": *landmarks*, *lead line*, and *log line*. He steered from landmark to landmark, checking them off on his chart (the sailor's word for "map"). Dropping a lead weight on a marked line (called "sounding") showed the depth of the water beneath the ship. From seabed samples, brought up on the tallow-filled base of the lead, an experienced navigator could tell where the ship was. Counting knots on the log line as it unreeled showed the ship's speed.

Out at sea, the navigator had to calculate the ship's *latitude*—its position north or south of the Equator. To do this he measured the sun's height above the horizon at noon, or that of the Pole Star at night, using an *astrolabe*, a *cross-staff*, or a *quadrant*. The east–west position or *longitude* was worked out using the distance sailed from the port of departure. *Compass* and log gave the direction and speed; time was measured by turning *sandglasses*.

A TRAVERSE-BOARD was used during each 4-hour watch to record changes of course. Working outward from the center, a new peg was put in every half hour to show the course being steered and help calculate the ship's position. Dividers were used to mark off equal distances on the chart. Time at sea was measured by turning sandglasses every 30 minutes.

USING THE "THREE Ls." Lookouts find shore landmarks, the lead line measures water depth, and the log measures the ship's speed. Speed was reckoned by counting the knots that ran out after the log had been dropped into the sea. Ship speeds are still measured in "knots" even today.

Log line and reel

Log

Hollow base full of tallow

Leads

A handsome 16th-century Italian compass with ivory case and lid

Traverse board

Sandglasses

Dividers